DIGGING TO THE PAST

DIGGING TO THE PAST

Excavations in Ancient Lands

W. JOHN HACKWELL

CHARLES SCRIBNER'S SONS / NEW YORK

Charles Scribner's Sons Books for Young Readers
Macmillan Publishing Company, 866 Third Avenue, New York, NY 10022
Collier Macmillan Canada, Inc.

Book design by Vikki Sheatsley   Printed in Japan by Toppan Printing Co.

First Edition   10 9 8 7 6 5 4 3 2 1

Library of Congress Cataloging-in-Publication Data
Hackwell, W. John.   Digging to the past.
    Includes index.
    Summary: Describes the routines of archaeological field work as participants painstakingly search for information about the past; and discusses some assumptions about life long ago in the Middle East, based on discoveries made there.
    1.Archaeology—Field work—Juvenile literature.
2. Civilization, Ancient—Juvenile literature. 3. Antiquities—Juvenile literature.
[1. Archaeology—Field work. 2. Civilization, Ancient]   I. Title.
CC76.H33 1986   930.1   86-13115   ISBN 0-684-18692-6

CONTENTS

Searching for Lost Worlds

1

Archaeology is often thought of as "treasure hunting" or searching for lost worlds. It really refers to the study of the remains of the past in order to see how ancient humans lived.

The idea of systematic study coupled with excavations did not arise until very recent times. Modern archaeologists and concerned citizens are appalled at the violence by which ancient treasures were uprooted from their buried homes in the past. In most cases all indications of the context of the finds were destroyed, making it impossible to understand their true artistic and cultural value.

The earliest excavations in the Middle East began in the nineteenth century, but they lacked any form of control of the information. The leaders simply excavated holes in the ground, using hundreds of local people working in mass confusion. It wasn't until the 1930s that a systematic archaeological project was undertaken by the University of Chicago at Megiddo, in Palestine.

Not all discoveries have been made by trained archaeologists. On a very hot day in 1880, a boy was playing near Jerusalem's old city and wandered into a dark tunnel. He slipped and splashed into a pool. When he stood up, he saw a Hebrew inscription that said: "King Hezekiah's Tunnel."

Just a few years ago, a shepherd boy named Muhammad Adh-Dhib tossed a stone into a remote cave beside the Dead Sea. He heard a sound like pots smashing to pieces. When he climbed in to investigate, he discovered jars and jars of scrolls—now known as the famous Dead Sea Scrolls, regarded by many scholars and historians as the single most important discovery of modern times.

Archaeologists today do not dig in the remains of ancient settlements simply in the hope of discovering treasures such as cult objects, beautiful pottery, or even rare scrolls, important as these finds are. Anthropologists have influenced archaeologists to become concerned with a much wider ancient environment.

Today archaeologists believe that the habits of ancient peoples—such as settlement, land use, and diet—have been determined by changing ways of obtaining food. This new understanding or theory, called the "food systems" approach to archaeology, lies at the basis of much modern archaeological research. Whereas the records of early western explorers through the Middle East seem little more than shopping lists for ancient treasures, today's archaeologists relate their work to the broader perspective of the food system. They are interested as much in the relationship between such matters as ancient waterworks, roads, terraces, and arrangements for preparing and storing food as they are in the architectural wonders and treasures that continually appear.

Modern archaeologists desire to understand more precisely the ancient agricultural and natural landscape, with particular interest in

Unique among research disciplines, archaeology destroys part of its context. Therefore, those involved in every excavation project must take accurate field notes on every aspect of the dig.

finding ancient forests, cereal fields, and orchards. They are also interested in a more precise study of ancient farming sites that were worked by one family and then abandoned. These "farmsteads" often differ widely in layout, land use, and structures such as wells, cisterns, and winepresses.

Another goal set by this approach is to recreate the ancient road systems and public waterworks, markets, and other communal undertakings. In other words, today's archaeologists don't simply ask: "What loot can we take back to our museums?" Instead they are interested to know if the ancient inhabitants were camel traders, sheep- or goatherders, or settlers and what environmental factors—such as rainfall and forestation—influenced their chosen life-style.

Many ancient communities had to guarantee access to water, especially in times of emergency. This was often attained by digging or cutting a channel to the water source.

The Expedition

2

A typical archaeological expedition to the Middle East has between 20 and 75 members, depending on the funds available and the extent of the project. It usually takes place during the summer vacation period and lasts from four to ten weeks.

Most archaeologists and their supporters depend on a separate source of income between excavation seasons. In other words, archaeologists are never made rich by excavating!

Heading the expedition is a director, generally a person who has experienced many seasons working "in the dirt" and who has a university degree in archaeology or a related field of study. Under the dig director is the chief archaeologist, who is responsible for the daily routine of digging at the chosen excavation site. An administrative director takes care of all the logistical matters such as transportation, payroll, employment of local workers, and equipment.

The Environmental Survey Team

The first of the three working groups of the expedition is the environmental survey team. Headed by an anthropologist, it includes an engineer, an aerial photographer, a helicopter pilot, a biologist, a lithicist (expert in the area of stone), a botanist, an ecologist, and—since the team will often enter private property on their survey—a local guide and translator.

A major objective of the survey team is to study the present environment of the region by collecting plants in the area and mapping local plant communities to study their succession patterns. This team will also study the soil and analyze the types, profiles, acidity, erosional patterns, and other features, such as water availability and drainage.

Another objective is to recreate the environment as it was throughout antiquity, and they achieve this by studying all animal remains found within their survey area. From this information they will know what conditions would have been needed to sustain these animals.

The aerial photographer locates ruins of rural buildings, such as walls, reservoirs, mills, wells, transportation networks, villages, and forests. On the ground, the survey team randomly samples all pottery, animal remains, loose artifacts, and other objects found lying on the surface.

The survey team will always refer to other information, such as ancient documents and inscriptions that have already been recovered from the area, in this way learning about the impact of the ancient environment upon the humans that inhabited the land.

The survey team will also study the way the present inhabitants live and work, since these observations will provide evidence concerning the ancient past. Anthropologists, for example, may live in a local village for some months, even years, taking notes on the lifestyles that they encounter.

The survey team works very closely together. Mornings are spent gathering data, and afternoons and evenings are spent at base camp comparing notes and analyzing infor-

Excavating creates continuous tension between the need to dig and remove and the need to preserve and isolate. Here the dig staff gathers among ancient ruins to discuss strategies for the coming activities.

mation. Nobody works independently in a survey, because the team has set itself the joint task of reaching a wide-ranging set of goals.

The Site Excavation Team

Old-fashioned "dirt" archaeology is still considered important to the broad objectives of the expedition, and the chief archaeologist leads a team of excavators whose primary aim is to uncover part of an ancient site.

While excavators are generally concerned with uncovering an ancient city, many concentrate on smaller undertakings such as a road, a cemetery, an isolated tomb or tower, or even a scattered ruin on a barren hilltop.

Throughout antiquity life was often taken up on the ruins of an abandoned village, and this process of settlement and abandonment repeated itself over the centuries, leading to the formation of large mounds or hills that had several occupation layers or strata filled with debris. These sites are called "tells."

The objectives of site excavation are to discover who occupied the site and under what circumstances they abandoned it. Excavators want to know how gifted the ancient inhabitants were in working with stone and other such materials and what can be understood about their diet, settlement arrangements, religious beliefs, burial practices, and hunting skills.

The team will also wish to ascertain the relationship between these city-dwellers and the people who occupied the surrounding region and farmlands that the ecologist in the team is surveying.

Unlike the survey team, the excavation staff must never forget that they will leave ugly deep holes in the ground when they have completed their task. If their excavation is to be successful, they must make meticulously accurate records, since future generations will have only those records if they are to understand anything of the ancient site.

The presence in the Middle East of the horse and cart is one of the more obvious examples of the way anthropological archaeologists make projections from the present to the past. The horse and cart of today is the descendant of the horse-drawn chariots of the ancient Egyptians and Syrians that were so effective in the open plains.

The Dig Support Teams

ECOLOGY

To support both the survey and excavation teams, the project establishes a temporary ecology laboratory at the base camp to provide in-field analysis of the inorganic and organic materials that are gathered.

Such a laboratory has several specialized stations. There is a geology station for examining rocks, soils, and bricks; a botany station to examine pollen, carbonized seeds, and living plant materials; an animal bone station to study skeletal remains of recent and ancient animals; a human bone station; a cartography station where detailed maps of the region will be prepared.

The maps record the physical features of the site and express the topographic contours and changes in elevation and surface. A finished map will show the locations of the test diggings as well as the locations of the deep trenches where the major excavating took place. Because this is a very complex and demanding task, the team secures the services of a professional surveyor.

The drafting team prepares a topographical map showing the areas that have been excavated.

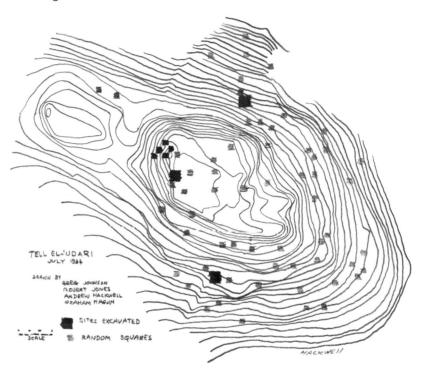

During one brief excavation season a dig team will take thousands of field photographs to ensure that records are kept of each aspect of the project.

This field laboratory also houses identification, documentation, and conservation facilities where pottery, flints, and other objects can be processed.

ELECTRONIC
DATA PROCESSING

All aspects of the survey and excavation have to be recorded and interpreted, and this is most effectively done with the aid of a computer system. The computer programmer not only creates the data base as the data are gathered but makes the data available on a daily basis to the specialists who lead the project.

All members of the expedition staff record their findings on computer-generated description sheets that have been designed with computer entry in mind.

TECHNICAL SERVICES

A technical services laboratory is also located at the base camp to coordinate the work of the photographers, draftspersons, and artists who are members of the expedition with the purpose of preparing the final publications or reports of the project.

The Dig
Gets Under Way

3

Since the weather is often extremely hot in the Middle East during the summer, the workday begins at 3:30 A.M. to avoid the heat of the afternoons. If the team is housed in temporary quarters, such as a government school, they will travel by chartered bus to the site each day. After working till 12:30 P.M., they will return to the base camp and spend the afternoon in a brief siesta, followed by various duties at the base camp laboratory.

Excavating is not a glamorous pastime. Daily work on the tell is the repetition of a small number of duties.

Surface Work

Before any digging begins, surveyors mark out the entire mound with six-by-six-meter (approximately 20 feet) squares using pegs and

The surface to be excavated must be thoroughly broomed before the square is probed.

strings. They also provide the team with a control point (called a "datum"), from which all measurements of the site will be taken. It is generally the highest point on the tell.

A typical tell may be assigned 10,000 such squares, with approximately 20 to be opened in any one season. Each of the squares will be excavated by a square supervisor and one or two assistants. Local Bedouin tribesmen are also employed in this capacity.

The first task of the square supervisor is to clean the square, using a brush and dustpan to sweep away all the loose stones and broken pottery lying on the surface.

Next, the soil on the surface is loosened with a large pick. The object is not to break it up at high speed but to soften it slowly while watching for skeletal remains or clay pots that may be hidden just beneath the surface. On some occasions an archaeologist has recovered the most important find from this surface soil—so right from the start everyone takes his or her role seriously.

The square supervisor is responsible for taking soil samples wherever changes in the

A young worker, using a hoe as a scraper, collects loose soil.

color or composition of the soil can be observed. Archaeologists wish to know what the soil is composed of and to what degree it is compacted. This information may offer a clue to the interpretation of the area.

Workers collect the loose stones lying about the surface and wheel them away from the excavation site while other staff members gather seed and plant remains for the laboratory.

Commencing the Probe

Once the surface material has been removed, a trench is dug in one of the corners of the square. Using a hand pick and a trowel, the worker peels away the soil layers, inch by inch, and carefully collects the loose dirt into rubber baskets called "guffahs."

The excavator can get the greatest control of his hands when kneeling in the trench. He uses the trowel to pull away the loosened soil after every two or three pick strokes. In this way he can see fully what each pick stroke is uncovering.

This is a very slow process, because the excavator must watch for rocks that are set in a row. Even if he finds only three small rocks, he must leave them in place and work around them, in case they are the top stones of a small wall or installation. Not until these stones have been completely undermined and the next layer exposed can the worker safely make a decision to remove them from the square.

Sometimes an archaeologist will find mud bricks, which were made in antiquity from clay and straw. These sun-dried bricks crumble very easily, and it may take a full day to uncover just five or ten such bricks.

Sifting

All of the soil collected in the guffahs has to be sifted through a fine mesh, a job that requires two people—one to shake the sifter and one to remove the large stones that could damage any delicate ancient objects that may have been collected in the probe.

Once the soil is completely sifted, the

Following the face of a wall down to its floor can be nerve-wracking. There is the ever-present danger of missing or cutting right through the floor.

sifters study everything that remains on the mesh—hoping always to find an ancient figurine or a knife or even a bone. Occasionally tiny beads and earrings are discovered by the people digging the square. Only the sifters can detect such small objects.

Pottery

Since pottery was cheap in the ancient world, people didn't bother to repair broken pots but threw them away, so the people working the sifts may discover thousands of pieces of broken pottery. It is the most common material saved from an excavation and has properties that make it of the greatest value to the archaeologist.

All the broken pieces of pottery are called "shards" and every piece has to be collected, counted, washed, and identified and mended as needed.

Shards are studied not just for their shape, coloring, or decoration, but for any writing that may have been scratched on the surface. Shards with such writing are called "ostraca."

The workers sieve debris through a fine mesh to ensure that all crucial artifacts, however small, will be retrieved.

These are so important that just one ostracon from an entire ten-year excavation project can be more valuable than any other find on the tell.

Cards 1 and 2 mark off each area separated by a hardened surface as the archaeologist continues to remove soil.

In the ancient world, a panel of judges would inscribe a piece of broken pottery when casting a ballot. If a defendant was found guilty as a result of the ballot, the judges would send the person away from the community. This was called "ostracizing," a word from which we derive our modern term for inscribed pieces of broken pottery.

Pottery does not deteriorate. Even if it is smashed to pieces it maintains its form, color, and texture. It can survive for thousands of years buried in a tell and yet, when washed and cleaned, will show most of its original luster.

In the ancient world pottery was subject to sudden changes of fashion, so the progression in time in any one settlement is mirrored by changes in pottery styles. Since shapes and decorations in each community were so distinct, they can be recognized wherever they are found.

Pottery can provide archaeologists with evidence of contact between communities—thus making it relatively easy to establish historical dates.

When no written documents are recovered, delicate and beautiful ceramic vessels such as these can help to fix the date of the ancient site.

Every bucket of pottery, flint, or other objects must be labeled each day in the field and later registered on the computer.

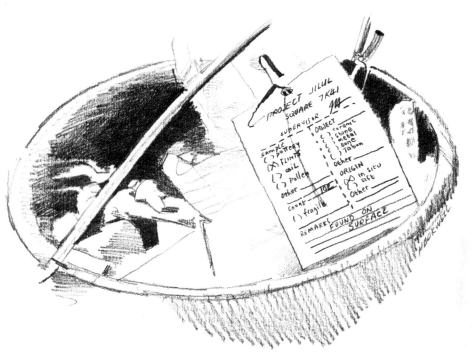

Once the pottery from the excavation site is returned to the field laboratory, archaeologists employ several techniques for understanding its significance. First they will study the formal attributes of the ware, such as its use and source of manufacture. Was it made using coils of clay or was it turned on a wheel?

When the excavation season is over, the team prepares a report for scholars. It includes cross-sectional drawings of all the pottery. The right side of each drawing indicates the thickness of the vessel, the left side its external shape and decoration.

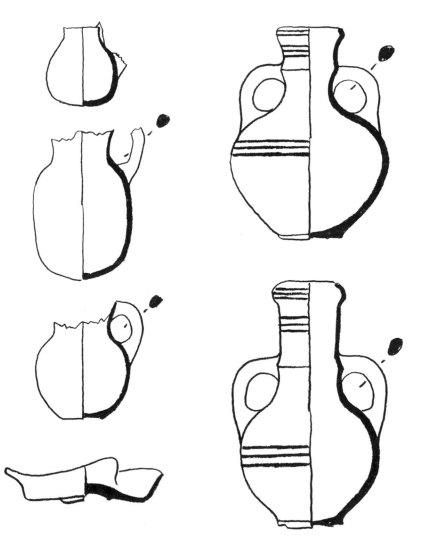

The next most important aspect of their study considers the distribution of the pottery in its context on the tell. What other items were found alongside the pot?

The laboratory technician in charge of the pottery materials sorts the ware on a table and classifies it according to type and location, thickness, and function.

Once the pottery has been through the several stages of classification, washing, and labeling, it is passed to the staff artist, who will draw it according to a rigid convention.

The potter was one of the most important people in an ancient village. He made bricks and tiles as well as huge vessels for carrying and storing water. (Even today archaeologists working for long hours in this hot environment find that their own drinking water remains very cool when stored in clay jars.) Women went to the well each day to collect the family supply of water and carry it back to the village. In the evening the family would bathe. Since there was only a small amount of water available, they washed standing up

It is the responsibility of the square supervisor to keep a record of the number of buckets of shards collected each day.

Taking a break from excavating, a worker drinks from a clay water pot like those of the ancients.

while a servant poured water over them and rubbed olive oil into their hair. Olive oil, stored in very small jars, was not only used as shampoo but was rubbed into burns and battle wounds.

Balks

As the excavators proceed deeper and deeper into the square, they preserve an unexcavated block one meter wide on the north and east sides. These walls are called "balks," and they play an increasingly important role as the archaeologist seeks to interpret his work.

These balks are kept perfectly vertical and as smooth as possible, since all changes in soil color and density can be easily recognized when studied. Archaeologists even speak of "reading" the balk. Such reading enables an archaeologist to tell if a soil layer has been windblown, laid down by water, or artificially filled to provide a new surface for the occupants at that stage.

Architectural Remains

Site excavators will often uncover huge masonry, such as boulder walls that have been erected to protect the ancient city. On a normal tell, the wall is built at a convenient location on the slope, and the top of the tell is usually the most strongly fortified internal area. Sometimes the inside of the wall is lined with benches or platforms that have surfaces of either brick or plaster. In ancient times the leaders of the city (called "elders") would sit there and watch for travelers entering the city through the complex arrangement of defensive gates.

The dig supervisor carefully records all the details of this stage of the excavation, looking for evidence of an ancient battle, such as fallen rocks or thick layers of ash or debris, which would suggest that an invading army set fire to the place. Slingstones are often found on the floor surface near such a defense wall.

To complete this part of the project, the supervisor will call on the assistance of the surveyors, to take levels and to draw sketches of every stone and boulder in its place. When an object is found standing in its place of origin, archaeologists refer to that object as *in situ*.

As probing continues, balks act as a vital guide to archaeologists.

Artifacts and Other Finds

4

U nderstanding the value of artifacts in ancient societies is essential to understanding ancient social life. Artifacts had a wide range of purposes as elements of the economy and as symbols of social status and religious beliefs. They come under several broad categories. There are ancient tools for food preparation, consumption, and storage. These include millstones, grinders, mortars and pestles, as well as various stone bowls.

There are finds that reflect industrial activity such as spindle whorls, spindles, loom weights, weaving spatulas, and chains. Architectural objects may include rope-stone weights used as counterweights for doors.

In the ancient world, figurines of stone, bone, and pottery not only reflect the development of a real artistic sense but also indicate a magic function in increasing fertility for people and for soil.

Every excavation has its quantity of luxury items, such as beads, pendants, bangles, earrings (mostly worn by the men), cosmetic palettes, and polished-metal mirrors. The discovery of a large quantity of these special items can indicate to the archaeologist that the ancient community was sufficiently wealthy to engage in extensive trade with neighbors.

Cult objects of bone, stone, or clay can shed light on the religious beliefs of an ancient community. In antiquity figurines representing the earth mother were used in rites aimed at increasing fertility in human beings and in the land.

Coins

Archaeological discoveries become increasingly important when they can be dated by means of the ancient coins found on a tell. The discovery of coins can also contribute immensely to the work of many people associated with the end result of a project.

For those studying history, for instance, a series of coins can become a list of ancient kings in the order of their reign. For the student of ancient writing (called an "epigrapher") the coins will provide clues to an

Both sides of the coins found in a dig are displayed in the final report. Likenesses of gods and goddesses were often depicted on coins. Top: Pegasus and Athena; center: Zeus and an eagle; bottom: Helios and a rose.

ancient alphabet. The art historian will be intrigued by the endless designs.

For archaeologists coins play a vital role in the dating of a particular event in antiquity. If, for example, a cache of coins lies among the debris of some intentional destruction level—such as a fallen wall or broken down temple—archaeologists can estimate the date of the destruction by the date that the coins were minted.

In the ancient world coins were not just money used for commercial transaction. They served the same function as a national flag does today. They indicate to us the independence and identity of a particular people or nation. When an ancient community minted its own coins, it signaled to the surrounding world that it was claiming independent status.

The symbols on ancient coins are the special study of numismatics. Symbols were devices used by the ancients to represent the mysterious forces of nature that surrounded them—thus providing them with a sense of security. Ancient people were concerned about the origin of things, and their rituals and festive celebrations revolved around the activities that sustain life, such as planting, fishing, hunting, harvesting, and gathering food—motifs often depicted on coins.

The migration of symbols is a unique story in itself. One can see that many foreign symbols were adopted, modified, and reinterpreted in a creative way that broadened religious concepts. Coins therefore played an important role in making diverse people aware of others' cultures.

When coins are discovered on a dig, there are always plenty of volunteers willing to clean and polish them and lay them out on velvet for the artists and photographers to study. All publications reporting an archaeological excavation proudly illustrate their coin finds in very neat rows.

Mosaics

Most ancient villages had their own temple or public meeting hall. These were not like today's temples, which seat thousands of people at one time, but rather like small bedrooms. One of the most interesting things about ancient temples was the floor. Often it was covered in a mosaic, and archaeologists feel very successful when they have uncovered a complete floor.

Animal pictures on mosaics tell much about the past. These will often include pictures of lions and antelopes, crocodiles, bears, and fallow deer—animals that once had been common in the region. Overgrazing by camels and especially goats, as well as the destruction of the forests for fuel, gradually deprived such animals of food and shelter, and often the only way archaeologists know that they once lived in the area is through the discovery of mosaics.

Ancient inscriptions, including place-names of cities, are sometimes found on mosaics, and of course this is a discovery of supreme interest to archaeologists.

Seals

One object that always causes great interest if found on an excavation is a king's seal. Such seals often tell more about the site than any other object.

In the ancient Near East, seals were cut in various types of stone or ceramic and engraved to establish ownership—of property, for instance—or the authenticity of a document.

Seals were also amulets meant to protect the wearer and bring good fortune. Seals therefore had a close relationship with their owners and were considered as integral a part of their owners' person as toenails!

Some seals were made by priestly scribes and combined religious ideas with everyday events. Other seals were inscribed with legal texts, court records, or loan documents, and as such they would describe the property, the price, and a statement of purchase.

Before seals were invented, ancients could impress a thumbnail in clay and this would bind an individual to a contract.

Almost everyone who could afford a seal could own one. There were low-priced "supermarket style" seals that were rather carelessly carved and mass-produced. Other seals, such as those made of stone for a king, were said to rival jasper and other precious gems in value.

Seals have been found that depict processions, offerings, drinking scenes, land-

The decorative patterns on mosaics provide archaeologists with an immediate visual presentation of life in the ancient world.

These seal impressions are actual size. Ancient Near Eastern officials sealed tablets, containers, and even storerooms with cylinders bearing their names and titles much the way customs officials bind and seal international shipments.

scapes, animals, and sacred trees, animals with human attributes, monsters with partially human features, composite animals, sundisks, chariots, altars, water, birds, reptiles, and dragons.

Medical Instruments

Through many excavations numerous medical and surgical instruments have been recovered. One of the first such instruments to be found by archaeologists was in use during the first century A.D. It was called a "gourd," after its shape, and it was employed in one of the most common of ancient operations. Believing the "humor" had to be extracted somewhat in the way you would extract a tooth, ancient physicians would heat the interior of these metal gourds and then place them against human flesh, believing that in this way they were thus sucking "humor" from the side of the afflicted person.

Treasures from Tombs   5

Cave and rock-shelter sites have special meaning to the excavation team because it is in places like these that ancient peoples buried their dead. Burial places are usually small and dark and often house a rich trove of treasures.

There are several distinctly different types of tombs represented in the Middle East, and they all tell us something about the people of antiquity. There is the familiar "rolling-stone" tomb—made famous by the tomb of Jesus in Jerusalem. There are cemeteries that have large, open tombs laid out in rows. There are chambers cut into the sides of a hill or cliff.

Some tombs have steeped entrances that descend to bedrock. Another style of tomb is the large hillside cave having two or more inner chambers called "vaults." These vaults are often lined with

The dig engineer uses highly sophisticated equipment to locate underground caves.

burial urns. Many have been blackened with soot from the campfires of wandering nomads who used the tomb as a shelter.

Wealthy people in antiquity were buried in caves on ledges. Such ledges had several corpses stacked together. Family burial caves were often so full of dry bones and offerings, such as beads and weapons, that some of the remains have been found pushed together to make room for more burials. Each time a cave was opened to bury someone, it had to be sealed again to prevent wild animals or dogs from consuming the newly buried body.

When a person died, everyone in the household, including the slaves, would cry aloud; some would even cut their arms with knives, pull their hair out, or cut off a finger, to show the family members how very sorry they were over the death. Some villages had professional mourners, who received payment for beating themselves in public at the time of the funeral.

The body would be washed and annointed

In some caves ancient people lived for extensive periods, leaving after them not only deep layers of debris but also human remains. Such finds indicate a development of burial customs and unmistakable ritual practices for the dead.

and dressed in the garments that the deceased was wearing at the time of death. At the height of Mesopotamian and Egyptian influence, the dead were often provided with food.

Sometimes archaeologists discover human bones stacked in clay pots. This is called a "secondary burial," since it is thought that nomads once buried their dead in a temporary tomb, later removing the bones and carrying them in earthen vessels as they traveled from place to place.

Some of the best evidence for the religious and social life of ancient people comes from the graves. When a grave is being uncovered, the excavator tries to expose several parts of the skeleton carefully. Dental picks, pocketknife blades, syringes, and small paintbrushes are useful for cleaning such fragile remains.

After identifying the critical points of the skeleton—such as the skull, pelvis, knees, and elbows—the excavator works carefully around the grave looking for any personal equipment such as spears, axes, or daggers. This task is not complete until all the soil around the bones has been removed and the photographers have taken pictures of the skeleton in the exact place where it was found.

Finally the excavator takes great care to re-

In preparation for burial the eyes of the deceased were closed, the mouth was often bound up, and the body was inspected as a precaution against burying somebody only seemingly dead.

This skeleton, found with an iron spearhead lodged in the neck, is presumably that of a warrior fallen in battle.

move the bones from the grave and transport them to the laboratory for further study and classification.

Large quantities of skeletal remains are stored for the duration of the dig, and a representative collection is shipped back to the sponsoring universities where the best finds are often used to recreate a burial chamber in a museum. All bones are available to students of archaeology and related fields.

Discovering the manner of burial, such as in an open series of graves, is often helpful to an excavation team since it is assumed that the people did not die all at once but somewhat in succession. Thus, burials like this can be placed in "order," and the objects from the tombs will often show a progression from primitive to more sophisticated.

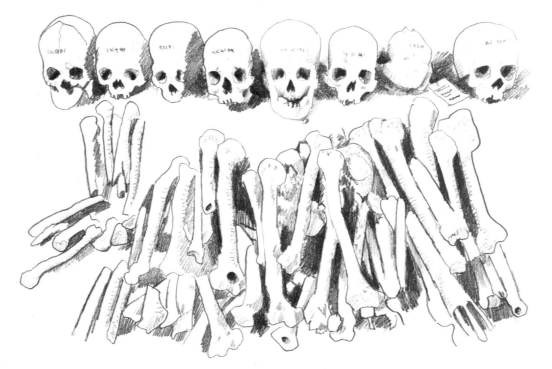

All human skeletal remains from an excavation are kept in storage for the duration of the project since archaeologists wish to determine if the ancient burial ground served only a local community or a much wider population.

Life on the Dig 6

An internationally reputable dig is certain to attract attention. The location of the dig, its significance for archaeological research, the reputation of key staff members—in particular, the director—are factors that draw applicants from all over the world.

Some volunteers may be college or university professors of archaeology who are seeking practical experience in the field. Others include graduate students looking for relevant thesis material. Middle East excavations attract seminary students who find in archaeology vital background to their theological studies. The majority of participants, however, are undergraduates who are taking credits in archaeology or related fields.

Other volunteers include retirees with no better qualification than a lifelong fascination with archaeology.

Approximately twelve months prior to departure, the expedition advertises in journals of archaeology, seeking volunteers for the dig. Participants are chosen for their interest, experience, and the dig's relevance to their particular academic pursuits.

Applicants will also be asked to list additional skills, such as carpentry, nursing, art, photography, architecture, or foreign language proficiencies, that would enhance their overall contribution.

The most indispensable qualification is an ability to adapt to the often harsh conditions that dig life demands, combined with a willingness to remain for the entire season.

Few people realize the hazards that such an expedition faces, especially when the team goes to a remote part of the Middle East. There is always the risk of illness from contaminated water or food prepared under unsanitary conditions.

The more fortunate digs are located near major cities where motel or hotel accommodation is readily available, and in these circumstances the dig staff has all the luxuries of home.

Others may have to locate in makeshift housing, such as a government school where cold showers and sleeping on hard floors are the norm. The more remote teams, however, must live in tents, enduring many inconveniences, such as no more than a flask of water for each member every day.

The biggest hazard during any excavation is the potential danger of lung congestion from the dust that blows everywhere, especially when working in dusty caves. For these and other reasons, most excavations take along a doctor and a nurse to provide basic medical care.

If the excavation is located in a remote area, archaeologists eat local food. Breakfast will usually include *fatteh*, flat bread dipped in *hummus*—a yogurt spread that is full of tasty cumin and freshly chopped parsley and other herbs.

Falafel is the favorite evening meal. It consists of flat bread filled with salad and beans

If a dig team is to be housed in tents, camp dangers are common, such as tripping over tent pegs and ropes and preparing food in field kitchens where mice and scorpions roam.

41

with plenty of freshly prepared goat's milk yogurt to make a satisfying meal.

Members of the staff must watch their own behavior so as not to offend the local people. In the Middle East, women's bodies are entirely covered, and in much of the area women also wear veils that hide their faces. For a westerner to work there clad only in shorts and a blouse, for instance, could offend the elders of the local village.

At the end of the digging season, the local people who have worked on the project may prepare a special farewell party called a *mensaf* for all the staff. This will include cooked lamb, literally covered in aromatic herbs and yogurt.

Such an occasion is very heartwarming, since the local helpers have established close bonds of friendship and commitment to the visitors who came to dig holes in or near their village. For some, this encounter could be the start of a serious future in archaeology. It is not unusual for archaeologists on a dig to employ a young Bedouin boy as a stone gatherer and to discover, some ten years later, the same person, having completed a university degree, representing his country in the Department of Antiquities.

Shopping for dig supplies is rather fun. Merchants display food and other goods under canvas in very narrow streets. Farmers, shepherds, and craftsmen come to these bazaars and sell the things they have grown or produced at home—jewelry, baskets, and water pots—along with imported transistors and mini-calculators.

7

Dividing the Finds

In the final days of the excavation, the team will not attempt to make any new probes or to open more tombs that may need several weeks to complete.

These final days have greater significance for the laboratory staff than for others attached to the project. The photographers will be rushing to complete their inventory of the objects collected; the various registrars will hurriedly record the finds that were uncovered in the last days of excavating; the dig director will busy himself laying out the most important finds in preparation for inspection by the local government; the administrative director will have his hands full caring for last-minute logistical needs.

Most excavation projects receive a permanent representative of the local government, a person who lives and works with the dig staff for the entire excavation season. It is that person's responsibility to protect the interests of his or her country.

On an appointed day at the end of the season, a group of government representatives comes to the base camp to inspect the physical results of the excavation and to determine which finds should remain in the country and which may be taken away. The day of inspection can be particularly unnerving to a dig director. Not only does he have a commitment to honest scholarship, but he is also aware that his private sponsors and donors back in his home country are eagerly hoping that he will return with exotic artifacts for display. Under most circumstances it is the local governments that determine the future of the rarer artifacts and other finds that have been recovered from the ground. Visiting expeditions cannot expect more than permission to show these finds for a limited season at a special display back home.

With the inspection completed, the project members prepare to return home where they can look forward to the extremely long process of cataloging and illustrating every aspect of the season's work.

Archaeologists make field notes at the conclusion of a day on the tell.

45

Key members of the team, such as the chief archaeologist and the anthropologist, as well as various square supervisors, will combine their resources to prepare a preliminary report on all the significant aspects of their expedition. This report may take a full year to write, edit, and have published in a journal on archaeology.

At the end of the season the excavation team hires heavy equipment to remove hundreds of tons of unwanted silt from the tell.

8 The Task Ahead

We hardly need to be reminded of the tremendous impact that the results of archaeology have on the modern world. The chief benefit of this very expensive exercise is to make the ancient past more vivid and real. Ancient Egyptians are seen eating, hunting, feasting, working, bewailing their dead. Nomadic tribes in Trans-Jordan are seen inhabiting the vast wastelands once thought to be barren, useless fields that did not support life in any way.

For archaeology there are yet many tasks ahead. Hundreds of sites remain to be explored—especially in Jordan, Saudi Arabia, and Turkey, where political and geographical considerations have made progress rather slow.

More and more universities today are making generous grants available for the extension of this valuable field of study. Perhaps one day you too will share in the thrill of discovery as you take a trowel and a pick to the ancient Near East in search of the lost wonders of the dead.

INDEX

archaeological dig: cataloging of an, 45–47; concluding inspection of the, 45; life on the, *40 ill., 42 ill.*; living conditions at the, 41–43; participants in the, 39; preparation for an, 41 (*see also* ecology laboratory, electronic data and processing, environmental survey team, Middle East, site excavation team, tells)

areas of the site, *19 ill.*

artifacts, importance of, 27–28

balk (unexcavated portion preserved), 24, *25 ill.*

basket, rubber (guffahs), 17

brooming the site, *14 ill.*

burial places, importance of, 33–38 (*see also* family burial caves, graves, secondary burial)

coins, importance of, 28–29, *28 ill.*

computer programmer (*see* electronic data and processing)

Dead Sea Scrolls, 2

destruction of context on site, *3 ill.*

ecology laboratory on site, 11–12

elders (city leaders), 25

electronic data and processing on site, 12

environmental survey team on site, 6–9

epigrapher (student of ancient writing), 28

excavations, 1–2, 9; problems between removing and preserving on site of, *7 ill.*

falafel (bread filled with salad and beans), 41–43

family burial caves (with "vaults"), 33–34; equipment used to locate, *34 ill.*; human remains in, *35 ill.*; *36 ill.*

fatteh (flat bread), 41

field notes, *45 ill.*

figurines, *27 ill.*

food systems approach, 2–4

future exploration, 48

gourd (*see* medical instruments)

graves, importance of, 36

guffahs (*see* basket)

Hezekiah's Tunnel, 2

hummus (yogurt spread), 41

in situ (object in its place of origin), 25

medical instruments, 32

mensaf (a farewell party), 42

Middle East, expeditions to the, 5; horse and cart in the, *8 ill.*; 19th-century excavations in the, 1–2; tombs in the, 33–36

mosaics, importance of, 29–31, *30 ill.*

olive oil, uses of, 24

ostracizing, 21 (*see also* pottery shards)

ostracon, ostraca (*see* pottery shards)

photographs as record of the day, *10 ill.*, 44

pottery, 19–24, *20 ill., 22 ill., 24 ill.*

pottery shards, importance of, 19–21, *23 ill.*; with writing (ostracon, ostraca), 19

probe, 17

rolling-stone tomb, 33

seals, importance of, 31–32, *32 ill.*

secondary burial, 36

site excavation team, 9

skeleton remains, found in family burial cave, *35 ill., 36 ill.*; of a fallen warrior, *37 ill.*; stored after excavation, *38 ill.*

slingstones, 25

soil, collection on site, *15 ill.*; sifting of, 17–19, *18 ill.*

surface work on site, 13–17, *14 ill., 15 ill., 16 ill.*

technical services on site, 12

tells, excavations of, 9, 13; final clearing of, *46 ill.*

topographical map on site, *11 ill.*

treasure hunting, archaeology as, 1

water sources for ancient communities, *4 ill.*